MRS MOLESWORTH

MRS MOLESWORTH

Mrs Molesworth

A WALCK MONOGRAPH

by

Roger Lancelyn Green

HENRY Z. WALCK, INCORPORATED
NEW YORK

Library of Congress Catalog Card Number: 64-20839
© The Bodley Head Ltd 1961
First American Edition 1964
Printed in Great Britain

CONTENTS

'We know an old-world garden of the mind
Where sweet tranquillity holds gentle sway;
And though tears come, the end is ever kind:
For there the summer smiles, and children play,
And life is fashioned in the quiet old way
Of simple pleasure and of sweet content.
In that kind garden many hours I've spent,
And almost wished my course had there been run;
Wherever *Mrs. Molesworth* led, I went,
To peace among her hundred books and one.'

A Note About the Author

A house full of books took the place of a more formal education for Roger Lancelyn Green until he went to Oxford, and interested him in those branches of literature and legend which he has made his particular study.

After taking his B.Litt., for which he presented a thesis on Andrew Lang, he was for a year a professional actor, one part he played being that of the pirate Noodler in *Peter Pan*—which led to the writing of *Fifty Years of 'Peter Pan'*. He was also an antiquarian bookseller and Deputy Librarian at Merton College, Oxford, before settling at Poulton-Lancelyn, the manor house where his ancestors have lived for nine hundred years. Since then he has written several adventure stories for children, some of them set against a background of Greek mythology. However, his interest in legend is not confined to Greece, and he has retold *King Arthur and his Knights of the Round Table*, *Robin Hood* and *The Saga of Asgard*.

While holding a Fellowship in English Literature at Liverpool University Roger Lancelyn Green edited *The Diaries of Lewis Carroll*, having already written *The Story of Lewis Carroll* for children and *Tellers of Tales* and other works on famous writers for children— amongst whom Barrie, Carroll, Lang and Mrs. Molesworth have been favourites for many years.

Acknowledgments

When Mrs. Molesworth died in 1921 her popularity was suffering from a temporary eclipse which even excluded her from *The Dictionary of National Biography*, and her daughter Olive, the only person fully competent to write of her mother, died without leaving reminiscences. In 1938 Miss Ruth Robertson began collecting such material as could still be gleaned, Mrs. Molesworth's daughter Cicely and her favourite cousin, the Hon. Mrs. Dyson-Laurie (Gwen Molesworth), being still alive. But her work was interrupted for ten years by the War in 1939, and her full-scale biography is still in preparation. Meanwhile, however, she has generously allowed me full access to a sheaf of precious letters and notes from friends and relatives now mostly dead, to add a personal touch to this little study and fill out many details in a rather cryptic life. Her thanks for this material—and the gratitude of all who are interested in Mrs. Molesworth—must here be expressed both to such members of Mrs. Molesworth's own family as the late Mrs. Prinsep (Cicely), the Hon. Mrs. Dyson-Laurie, Mrs. V. M. Inglefield, Mrs. Grant Bruce, Mrs. V. V. Browning, General E. C. Walthall, and Colonel F. C. Molesworth; such friends of hers as the Misses Du Cane, Mr. Ronald Noel Paton, Mrs. A. R. Craik, Mrs. Roscoe, Miss Surridge, Mr. A. P. Rogers and Mr. David Williamson; and the Librarian and staff of the Manchester Public Libraries, the Town Clerk and City Surveyor of Manchester, the Librarian of Dunfermline Public Library and Messrs Macmillan & Co. Ltd.—

and all others who for the past twenty-two years have helped Miss Robertson in her researches.

I must, however, take full responsibility for my interpretation and use of the material, and for the assumptions and generalizations which so short a work as the present renders inevitable. I, like so many others, wait with eagerness and impatience for Miss Robertson's detailed study of a fascinating character and an enthralling story-teller.

My own researches, though of almost as long standing as Miss Robertson's, have led me mainly among printed sources. Here the most important discoveries have been four autobiographical articles from which I have quoted freely, namely 'On the Art of Writing Fiction for Children' (*Atalanta*, May, 1893), 'How I Write My Children's Stories' (*Little Folks*, July, 1894), 'Story-Writing' (*The Monthly Packet*, August, 1894) and 'Story-Reading and Story-Writing' (*Chambers's Journal*, 5 November, 1898).

My personal debts, after the first and greatest to Miss Robertson, are to my mother for keeping her copy of *The Carved Lions*, her own childhood's favourite, to be my own introduction to Mrs. Molesworth (along with *Carrots* and *Us*) before I was ten; to the late Mrs. Lionel Molesworth, Mr. and Mrs. H. D. Molesworth, Mr. C. L. S. Cornwall-Legh, Miss Marghanita Laski, and the present occupants of 92 Rusholme Road and Tabley Grange.

R.L.G.

1. Little Miss Stewart

Mrs. Molesworth was one of the most autobiographical of writers and yet as elusive as her own Cuckoo: she based many of her best books on her own recollections, and particularly those of her childhood—but she can seldom be accepted as a true witness without independent support, and it is not always easy to be sure when all her fictional additions and alterations have been pruned away. Nevertheless she is her own best advocate wherever permissible, for she was endowed with an amazingly retentive memory: were it not that she could recapture the precise sensations of childhood, she would never have achieved her place among the great writers for children.

'The very first thing that I remember,' she wrote in 1894 in one of her few intentionally autobiographical essays, 'is a storm of wind. . . . Next comes a vision I have never, curiously enough, been able to localize. I am walking along an unevenly paved road; the large round cobble stones are trying to my little feet, and very slippery. I think they are wet with a coating of greenish seaweed; and though I cannot recall any consciousness of the sea, I think it must have been near, for the strong scent of tar is over all, and in front of me at one side stands the chief feature of the scene—rows and rows of masts stretching up, up, till to my fancy they are lost in the clouds.'

This fits exactly with her birthplace, West Nieuwland D.75, in Rotterdam, Holland, which was in a cobbled street just round the corner from one of the biggest and busiest of the canals: but she hesitated to accept the testimony of her memory since she left Holland, never to return, just before her second birthday.

Mary Louisa Stewart was born in this unexpected setting at noon on the 29th of May, 1839, being the eldest daughter and second child of Charles Augustus Stewart (*c.* 1809-1873), Merchant, by his wife Agnes Janet, *née* Wilson, (1810-1883). The marriage took place about 1835, and the eldest son, John Wilson Stewart, preceded Louisa by three years. After another three-year gap she was followed by Charles (1841), Agnes (1845), William (1846), and Caroline Marion (*c.* 1850). All her brothers died in early manhood, and only Charles left children—the Morier and Noel of the dedication to *Carrots.*

Charles Augustus Stewart was the son, or adopted son of Major General Stewart of Strath, Caithnesshire, a descendant of an Appin Stewart who fought at Culloden. General Stewart served with distinction through the Peninsular wars, and was rewarded by a grant of land in New South Wales, where he settled and held high administrative office. The General wanted Charles Augustus to follow a military career, but apparently some quarrel arose between them, and the young man threw up his Commission in the Buffs, and decided to carve out a livelihood for himself in commerce. Eventually he prospered so well that he became a senior partner in the Manchester firm of Robert Barbour Bros., Merchants and Shippers, with a considerable fortune to his credit.

When he settled in Manchester in 1841, however, he was only at the beginning of his career. Louisa's childhood was passed in anything but gilded halls, since she lived in the middle of Manchester until she was about fourteen, and then only in a suburb until her marriage at the age of twenty-two.

The home that she remembered best, 'only a rather small and dull house in a dull street'—86 Bloomsbury, Rusholme Road, (now 92 Rusholme Road)—is, we may assume, the one described in *Little Miss Peggy* and *The Carved Lions*. It was about three-quarters of a mile from the centre of Manchester, well in Smokytown by 1841, with slum houses and tenements across the narrow street below the back windows, even if the low hills of Cheshire were visible over the roof tops from the nursery windows on the top floor in front. Like the children in *Little Miss Peggy*,

'The children looked out on to a commonplace street, houses on both sides, though just opposite there was a little variety in the shape of an old-fashioned smoke-dried garden. Beyond that again, more houses, more streets, stretching away into suburbs, and somewhere beyond all that again the mysterious, beautiful, and enchanting region which the children spoke of and believed in as "the country", not really so far off after all, though to them it seemed so. And above the tops of all the houses, clear though faint, was now to be seen the outline of a range of hills, so softly grey-blue in the distance that but for the irregular line never changing in its form, one could easily have fancied

13

it was only the edge of a quickly passing ridge of clouds.'

As for Louisa herself, we have an even clearer picture of what she was like in the Bloomsbury days, derived from her very first story for children, 'The Reel Fairies', which opens *Tell Me a Story* (1875). This book was made up of stories and recollections told to her own children and, as it was published under a pseudonym, she did not even need to disguise her own name when telling of her childhood.

'Louisa was a little girl of eight years old . . . She was nothing particular to look at; she was small for her age, and her face was rather white, and her eyes were pretty much the same as other people's eyes. Her hair was dark brown, but it was not even curly. It was quite straight-down hair, and it was cut short, not *quite* so short as little boys' hair is cut nowadays, but not very much longer. Many little girls had quite short hair at that time, but still there was something about Louisa's that made its shortness remarkable, if anything about her could have been remarkable! It was so very smooth and soft, and fitted into her head so closely that it gave her a small, soft look, not unlike a mouse . . .

'Her home was not in the country: it was in a street in a large and rather smoky town. The house in which she lived was not a *very* pretty one; but on the whole it was nice and comfortable, and Louisa was generally very well pleased with it, except now and then, when she got little fits of wishing she lived in some very beautiful palace sort of house, with splendid rooms, and grand staircases, and gardens and fountains, and I don't know all what—just the same sort of little fits as she sometimes had of wishing to be very pretty, and to have lovely dresses, and to be admired and noticed by everyone who saw her. She never told anyone these wishes of hers: perhaps if she had it would have been better, but it was not often that she could have found anyone to listen to and understand her; and so she just kept them to herself.

'There was one person who, I think, could have understood her, and that was her mother. But she was often busy, and when not busy, often tired, for she had a great deal to do, and several other little children besides Louisa to take care of. There were two brothers who came nearest Louisa in age, one older and one younger [John, three years older; Charles, two years younger], and two or three mites of children smaller still [Agnes, six years younger; William seven—and later Caroline, eleven years younger]. The brothers went to school, and were so much interested in the things "little boys are made of", that they were apt to be rather contemptuous to Louisa because she was a girl, and the wee children in the nursery were too wee to think of anything but their own tiny pleasures and troubles. So you can understand that though she had really everything a little girl could wish for, Louisa was sometimes rather lonely and at a loss for companions, and this led to her making friends in a very odd way indeed. If you guessed for a whole year I do not think you would ever guess whom, or I should say *what*, she chose for her friends. Indeed, I fear that when I tell you you will hardly believe me; you will think I am "story-telling" indeed. Listen—it was not her doll, nor a pet dog, nor even a favourite pussy-cat—it was, they were rather, *the reels in her mother's work box*.'

In her autobiographical essay 'Story-Writing' in 1894 Mrs. Molesworth confirms this strange friendship, noting that she never cared much for big dolls, but only for little ones which could be grouped into families and made to play a part in dramatic stories. When dolls proved too few, the reels augmented their numbers, and further substitutes were found in a collection of rare shells.

'I almost think I preferred these substitutes for dolls, at one time, to the dolls themselves', she remembered. 'They allowed, the shells especially, such an unlimited scope for the imagination . . . I have sobbed for hours at the loss or breakage of some special favourite, a *prima donna* of my baby dreams.'

Just as the cotton-reels were celebrated in *Tell Me a Story*, so the shells gave the basis for another early story, 'My Pink Pet' (*Aunt Judy's Magazine*, Nov. 1877; collected in *A Christmas Posy*, 1888), though more fictional licence was given here to the facts, since Lois the little heroine has elder sisters.

A secondary incident in this story becomes the main-spring of another, 'The Goblin Face' (*Child's Pictorial*, Oct. 1885; collected in *Five Minutes Stories*, 1888). The background details are different—the little girl visits an uncle in a big house in Scotland, instead of an aunt in a small house by the seaside—but again she wakes at night to be frightened almost into hysterics by a large china jar on a high shelf which in the half-light takes on the appearance of a ghostly white face. Such fears trouble many an imaginative and sensitive child, and Mrs. Molesworth (who also used them with greater detail in her first novel) writes of them with an understanding that shows a vivid recollection of her own childish experiences.

These 'bugs that fright us' might have become apparent anywhere, but Louisa's 'Goblin Face' seems to have been located in an old country house, a few miles from Dunfermline, the home of an uncle and Mrs. Stewart's mother. Her visits there were among the highlights of Louisa's childhood. The 'Grandmother Dear' who helped to make them memorable was Mary, *née* Black (1765-1849), widow of John Wilson of Transy, Fife. His father, also John Wilson, was Provost of Dunfermline (1801-1808), and his wife Louisa's great-grandmother, was the owner, we may assume, of the curious old 'toon hoose' described in 'Grandmother's Grandmother' in *Grandmother Dear*.

'Grandmother's Grandmother' tells of incidents in the childhood of Louisa's mother, Agnes Janet Wilson. Here she is disguised as 'Nellie', but she appears under her own name in 'Mary Anne Jolly' in *Tell Me a Story* and 'A Long Ago Story' in *Carrots*. The stories are both about 'Janet', the youngest of the family, and Hugh who comes next in age, but 'died in the prime of his youthful manhood'.

Many things about Janet's mother, this 'little old lady' her Scottish grandmother, impressed Louisa strongly, and numerous tiny incidents in her books can be traced back to her recollections of the annual visits between 1841 and 1848. The old custom of the lady of the house washing the best china, for example, is specifically described as done by 'Miss Janet's mother' in *Carrots*, and occurs at greater length and most lovingly described in *Us: An Old Fashioned Story* (1885) which is set in the early years of the nineteenth century.

Of more importance were Grandmother Wilson's unrivalled powers of story-telling. Louisa describes the old lady and her stories at some length in an article in *Little Folks* (July, 1894):

'She seemed to me very old—more like a *great* grandmother; and so she was, for I was one of the youngest of a large group of grandchildren ... We were very fond of her, but just a little afraid of her too. She was so delicate and dainty; her hands, I remember, were particularly small, and everything about her was always so beautifully neat and precise that we never thought of rushing in to her with untidy hair or crumpled pinafores ... I can see her now, sitting in her favourite window, looking out on the lawn of a very old country house in Scotland, with my brothers and myself, and later on a little sister, round her in a group, while she told us "The Fair One with Golden Locks", or "The Brown Bull o' Norrowa", and sometimes stories of herself or her own children when they were young.'

18

When the visits to Scotland ceased, it fell to Louisa to remember and repeat to the younger children all that she could of Grandmother Wilson's stories—and doubtless to describe in more and more glowing terms the lost holiday home most of them had never known, and the country which to a town child in the days before motor transport was a rare and precious memory.

'The country was almost the same as fairyland to me,' says Geraldine in *The Carved Lions*, 'the peeps I had of it now and then were a delight I could not find words to express'. This magic of the country is conjured up and lingered over in story after story, and we catch many glimpses of the child confined to dark, smoky Manchester striving to reach the 'Delectable Mountains' so tantalisingly visible from the nursery window in Rusholme Road. Little Miss Peggy in her attempt to reach them found only a gaunt wood and a blackened meadow; a longer walk could still take Louisa and her mother to little villages only half swallowed up by the red tentacles of the advancing city: Fallowfield, for example, which is probably the 'Daisyfield' described so lovingly in her last full-length book, *The Story of a Year* (1910) when Fulvia and her mother walk to it from Miss Leinster's grim house in 'Northborough'.

Louisa's glimpses of the country after the long Scottish visits ceased were probably as few and precious as Geraldine's; but she was not altogether deprived of holidays, for the Stewarts managed to send their children to the seaside, though the place chosen had few country attractions. It is described in *Carrots* as:

'not what is called "picturesque": it was a long flat stretch of sandy shore, going on and on for miles just the same. There were very few trees and no mountains, not even hills. In summer a few, just a very few, visitors used to come to Sandyshore for bathing; they were always visitors with children, for everyone said it was a nice safe place for little people.'

The place described is Fleetwood on the Lancashire coast: 'Sandyshore', noted an interviewer in *The Quiver* in 1906, 'is a reminiscence of Mrs. Molesworth's own childhood, a seaside place where her parents had a little house, and where they used to send their children for some part of the year.'

'A dull, old-fashioned little seaside town,' Louisa calls it in another story, 'which we children thought paradise'. This paradise lost many of its charms as she grew older and missed the real country more keenly, but the fascination of the sea and the superb sunsets remained, while the lighthouse, the harbour, the long sand-dunes and the bleak coast stretching from the 'Parade' round the corner of the headland towards Rossall gave the setting for *The Rectory Children*, as well as the more general background of *Carrots*.

With Dunfermline and Fleetwood leaving such golden memories, it seems strange that Louisa's period at boarding-school at Lausanne in Switzerland when she was about fourteen is nowhere reflected in her stories. Switzerland is never mentioned, but boarding-school is so vividly described in *The Carved Lions* that it seems highly probable that in this very autobiographical story the Swiss school is merely moved back to Manchester to become the 'Green Bank' of Geraldine's ordeal.

Louisa's own education was almost entirely private, like Geraldine's.

'I cannot in the very least remember learning to read,' she tells us in one of the autobiographical essays, 'nor can I recall a time when reading stories was not my greatest delight, nor can I remember ever being unable to understand French or to speak it after a fashion . . . Though for all I can remember to the contrary, I learnt to read without the slightest difficulty or distress, this was by no means the case with writing. It was wretchedness and misery to me . . . I did not take kindly to Latin; I was intensely dull at arithmetic, and yet I loved it. Figures have always meant something inexpressible to me—every number had its individuality.'*

In her earlier years her mother was her only tutor, being an unusually well-educated woman who had spent some time in France and probably had distant relations in that country. We do not know whether Louisa ever had a governess; but she certainly had lessons besides those given by her mother and may have been a day pupil for a short time at some school in Manchester which cannot now be identified. If so, 'Green Bank' may owe something to this school as well as to the one at Lausanne, which followed it, and the school if not the

*The individuality of figures and letters is described at some length in the account of Helena's lessons in *My New Home* (1894) written in the same year as the article quoted above.

actual events may be represented in the story 'Poor Miss Crawfurd' (*Little Folks*, Nov.-Dec. 1889; collected with *The Story of a Spring Morning*, 1890).

After her return from what seems to have been a short and unsatisfactory period in the Swiss boarding-school, Louisa became one of the select few who attended private classes held by the Reverend William Gaskell, husband of the author of *Cranford*. It may even be that she received some tuition, before the Swiss interlude, from Mrs. Gaskell herself.

The Gaskells were near neighbours of the Stewarts, who moved from Rusholme Road to 77 Dover Terrace, Upper Brook Street, in 1853, and Louisa followed happily in the footsteps of the Winkworth sisters, and may have overlapped with some of them.

'It was under Mr. Gaskell's guidance,' wrote Susanna Winkworth of her sister Catherine, 'that she gained her wide knowledge of English literature, and her keen appreciation of style. Her own mind was stimulated by his rich and varied culture, rare critical power, and exquisite refinement of taste.'

This might have been said with equal truth of Louisa Stewart, who herself commented on 'the exceptional excellence' of William Gaskell as a teacher, 'himself a perfect master of style, a writer far less known by name than he deserved to be.'

Altogether Louisa's childhood in Manchester, though strictly organised and narrow in some respects, seems to have been an essentially happy one.

'What matters most to children is not *where* their home is, but *what* it is,' she makes Geraldine say in *The Carved Lions*, 'and our home was a very sweet and loving one, though it was only a rather small and dull house in a dull street. Our father and mother did everything they possibly could to make us happy. . . . '

Many more of Geraldine's recollections of her early days must be direct scraps of Louisa's own autobiography: old Miss Fryer the Quakeress and the special expeditions to her confectionery shop with 'mamma', with the loving details of purchases; the occasional visits to the bigger and more 'up to date' grocer; even perhaps the mysterious delights of Mr. Cranston's furniture shop—where it is hard not to believe that the two Carved Lions stand on guard to this day.

Meanwhile Louisa's father was prospering among the merchant princes with whom he had allied himself. The senior partner, Robert Barbour, was able to purchase Bolesworth Castle in Cheshire in 1857 and give up active participation in the firm of Barbour Brothers not long afterwards. Charles Augustus Stewart progressed more gradually: in 1855 he moved to 'The Croft', Carlton Road, Whalley Range, and some six years later to 'Whalley House'. Though still on the edge of Manchester, 'Whalley Range was a suburb of exquisite beauty', according to William Edwin Adams, who wrote of Manchester at about this date. It was not until after Louisa's marriage in 1861 that her father, like so many other successful business men of the period, was able to rent an old county seat from its impoverished owner and write himself as 'of West Hall, High Legh' in 1869 and for a few years following.*

The happy childhood in Manchester was marred a little by Louisa's sufferings 'from excessively Calvinistic surroundings', which, as she told Helena Swan (*Girl's Christian Names*, 1900, p. 355), made her 'determined that no child with whom she was brought in contact should, if she could prevent it, be taught the religion of fear'. From this resulted her consistent practice of making Sundays as pleasant as possible for the children in her stories. Her own creed became that of the Church of England, moderate and broad-minded, though turning towards Anglo-Catholicism in her old age.

But she was a pious child, and writes amusingly about a story-book of her early years, *The Fairchild Family*:

'my favourite by far, excepting for the prayers and hymns at the end of each chapter. These I was too conscientious to "skip", but they were a sore trial, till at last I hit upon the plan of *reading forward* a certain number of them, so that then I could go back and enjoy the story straight on for several chapters without the uncongenial break!'

*The fact that Mrs. Molesworth lived in Manchester until she was twenty-one, only leaving it for holidays at Dunfermline and Fleetwood, and for her short period of schooling in Switzerland, is stressed here, since Marghanita Laski has stated so definitely in her *Mrs. Ewing, Mrs. Molesworth, and Mrs. Hodgson Burnett* (1950), pp. 56-7 that 'Her childhood was spent in High Legh in Cheshire . . . she did *not*, like [Geraldine etc.] live in Smokytown but in the country'.

Other childhood reading which she mentions included Maria Edgeworth's stories, but 'there was something hard and dry about them, something wanting, which I could not define: they were too *sensible*'; *Evenings at Home* (1892-6, by Mrs. Aitken and Mrs. Barbauld); *Ornaments Discovered* (1819, Mary Hughes); *Jemima Placid* (n.d. Dorothy Kilner, 1755-1836); *Leisure Hours* (1795, Priscilla Wakefield); *The Twin Sisters* (c. 1812, Elizabeth Sandham), and several others.

Far more congenial were the fairy stories—'and the children of my day were very favoured as regards fairy tales. Grimm, and still more, Hans Andersen, were a library in themselves,' while *The Wonder Book*, *Tanglewood Tales*, *The Heroes* and *Heroes of Asgard* were published just in time for her. Her favourites were 'one perfectly delicious little fat brown volume' which 'contained *all* the dear old stories and some that are now forgotten, told in the true narrative style, minus aphorisms or lectures', and E.T.A. Hoffman's *Nutcracker and Mouse King* (probably in Mrs. St. Simon's 1853 translation).

Later came the works of Charlotte Yonge 'which seemed to open a new world of fiction, as indeed they did, especially, I think, the historical ones'; Elizabeth Sewell's *Laneton Parsonage*, and finally *The Wide, Wide World*—'I think I loved it better than any other storybook', she wrote in 1898: 'While I was reading it I seemed actually to live in the story', as she makes Geraldine say in *The Carved Lions*.

But she was also reading and revelling in the Waverley Novels from a surprisingly early age, and remembered when she was six being found in tears in her uncle's bookroom with her head on *Pevril of the Peak* 'because I *couldn't* understand the story; it got so muddled after the beginning. And *Ivanhoe* and *The Talisman*, and even *Anne of Geierstein*, were so much nicer and easier.'

Reading stories, telling stories to the younger children, and making up little charades for them to act, prepared Louisa Stewart for her future career. But she had no idea of this, even in her teens when she began submitting stray pieces to various periodicals, which cannot now be traced.

'The first thing I ever published was not original but a translation', she records. 'But it was very delightful to see my own words in print, and from this time I began sending trifling things to magazines—for no pay in those days, but just for the pleasure of their appearance.'

Probably there were few of these juvenile publications, and they are likely to have ceased altogether when Louisa 'came out' at seventeen or eighteen.

Although as a child she was 'small for her age', and in her own estimation at least, 'nothing particular to look at', she grew into a tall, good-looking woman. She had been given a more extensive education than most girls of her period, but her interests were by no means exclusively intellectual: she was a good horse-woman and a graceful dancer. We may assume that she had played some part in the social life in which the Gaskells and such friends as Professor Crawford Williamson of Owens College moved, though the only close friend of her own of whom we know anything was Ennis Graham, the explorer's daughter, who vanished in central Africa with her father. But it is probable that Louisa Stewart, when she first met her future husband, was still rather ingenuous and unsophisticated.

II. Major and Mrs Molesworth

It is not certain when Louisa Stewart first met Richard
Molesworth, but they probably became engaged about
1858, when Richard was home on leave after the Indian
Mutiny. One of their descendants has a sword engraved
with their joint initials which she is said to have given
him as an engagement present.

Richard Molesworth was the eldest son of Captain
Oliver Molesworth, R.A., third brother of the seventh
Viscount Molesworth of Swords and Baron Phillipstown
of Phillipstown in Ireland. He became an Ensign in the
19th Regiment of Foot (1st Yorks. N. Riding) on 23
November, 1854 and was promoted Lieutenant on 9
March of the following year. He served with his regiment in the Crimea from May, 1855, being engaged in
the attack on the Quarries on 7 June, and in the attacks
on the Redan on 18 June and 8 September. In the last
of these engagements he was severely wounded in the
head by shrapnel—which the medical science of the day
was not able to remove completely. Decorated with the
Medal and Clasp, and the Turkish Medal, he proceeded
with his regiment to India, returning home finally in
1860 and being promoted Captain on 4 June, 1861, with
which rank he transferred a month later to the Royal
Dragoons.

From all accounts he was a man of great personal
charm. 'Young, handsome, gallant—what girl could
have resisted him!' Louisa's youngest sister, long after,
told her great-niece, convincing her that 'it was a most
real love match: she loved Richard dearly and they were

young and happy together, whatever happened later.'

To outward appearances they were certainly a well-matched pair, but Louisa's mother had doubts about the suitability of the marriage, even though, at that time, Richard was heir presumptive to the Molesworth title. One of Richard's own relatives, a close friend of Louisa's, though of a younger generation, later explained the grounds for Mrs. Stewart's misgivings in the following manner.

'I never saw Major Molesworth, but Mrs. Molesworth told me herself that he had a very violent temper, and that her mother did not want the marriage for that reason; but she trusted to her own love and tact to keep it under control. She said it was due to the wound he had received in the Crimea on the top of his head.'

Though so gentle and yielding a character in some ways, Louisa could be determined and even headstrong when her deeper affections were involved: she disregarded her mother's warning and surrendered herself to love, under the conviction that it would conquer all difficulties. Later she could still recapture the first feeling of wonder and happiness in the opening stanza 'Spring' of her poem 'Nature and Love', published in 1875:

> 'The tender Spring comes tremblingly;
>   Quiv'ring the blossoms softly break;
> Each zephyr breathing gently by,
>   New forms, new beauties seem to wake.

So trembling wakes my love for thee,
So fetters burst, springs fair and free.
O first sweet love! O maiden mine!
O strange new love! O birth divine!'

The marriage took place on 24 July, 1861 at the
Grosvenor Square Church, Manchester, the Reverend
A. Monro, D.D., officiating, and the reception was held
at Charles Augustus Stewart's house in Carlton Road,
Whalley Range.

There is no record of a honeymoon, but it may have
been spent in Paris, if Mrs. Molesworth's apparently
very autobiographical third novel, *Not Without Thorns*
(1873), can be taken in evidence and, judging from the
same source, the young couple were already beginning
to find, before it ended, how disconcertingly unaware
they were of each other's real characters.

If disillusionment had already begun even during the
honeymoon, Mrs. Molesworth may have found the
thorns growing more apparent during the next few years
while she and her husband moved from place to place
with the Regiment. They were stationed at Dublin until
September, 1861, and thereafter at Birmingham until
May, 1863 when they moved to Aldershot: but apparently none of these places gave the background for any
of Mrs. Molesworth's stories, nor—unlike Mrs. Ewing,
the friend whose work she admired so much—do any of
her tales turn on Army life.

Only one incident has survived from these years: she
gave lessons in French and German to her husband's
batman, a gentleman ranker who afterwards achieved

fame as Archibald Forbes (1838-1900) the war correspondent and historian—who bears testimony in his memoirs to her charm as a tutor.

But more important were the births of their first two children, Agnes Violet Grace on 8 April, 1862 and Mary Cicely Caroline in December of the following year, for both of which confinements Mrs. Molesworth returned to her parents' home in Whalley Range.

Early in 1864 Richard Molesworth retired from the Regular Army with the rank of Major, and £1,800 in lieu of his Commission, probably on account of his health, which seems to have been deteriorating. With some financial help from Charles Augustus Stewart, now an exceedingly wealthy man who was preparing to rent the West Hall at High Legh from Captain Egerton Leigh, Major Molesworth took Tabley Grange some six miles away.

The house, which still belongs to the Tabley Estate, is a long, low building, partly stone and partly stucco. Originally a small farmhouse, it has been built on to and altered at various dates; and some at least of the alterations were made by the Molesworths, or by Charles Stewart on their behalf. It stands back among trees and shrubs near the main road from Northwich to Manchester, little more than a country lane a century ago, though now loud with almost ceaseless traffic.

'The additions had not been badly managed,' wrote Mrs. Molesworth in one of the numerous stories which use Tabley Grange for background. 'There was no glaring incongruity between the new and the old, and already the busy, patient ivy was doing its utmost to soften with its veiling green all offensive contrasts. It was a roomy old house ... The passages and stairs were wide, and the rooms, though several were small, had thick walls and deep-set windows that gave one a pleasant feeling of space.'

Major Molesworth's retirement did not last twelve months, for in January, 1865 he was appointed Adjutant of the 6th Royal Lancashire Regiment of Militia. Later the same year, after they were well settled at Tabley Grange, another daughter, Juliet, was born; and in 1867 came Olive. 'I rather fancy daughters are in the ascendant!' wrote a Molesworth relative at the time, since Samuel Molesworth the next Viscount, was also producing a succession of daughters: but a son in 1868 ended Richard Molesworth's very slender chances of the succession.

The five years at Tabley Grange, though they ended in tragedy, must have been one of the pleasantest periods of Mrs. Molesworth's married life, if we can judge by the number of times it can be recognised in her stories. They slipped easily into the social life of the county, entertaining and being entertained by the Brookes of Mere Hall, the Leghs of High Legh, Lord de Tabley who became a close friend and was Cicely's godfather, his son the poet and novelist, and Edward Delves Wathall of Wistaston who married Mrs. Molesworth's younger sister, Caroline Marian, in 1870. On Sundays they would drive the five or six miles to Rostherne Church above the legend-haunted mere, where the

Vicar was Alfred du Cane, whose cousin Richard's wife became Mrs. Molesworth's closest friend in London nearly twenty years later. Knutsford was only three miles away, but Mrs. Molesworth does not seem to have taken kindly to the rarefied social atmosphere of the little town which Mrs. Gaskell had made famous as 'Cranford'; and indeed she pilloried it herself as 'Mallingford' in her first novel, though in later stories it is treated a little more kindly.

Rostherne is on the way to High Legh, and when the Stewarts had settled at the West Hall, the two parties could meet at church and return thither for the rest of the day. The visits seem to have been frequent, and at Christmas it was the custom for the Molesworths to stay for several days.

At Easter, 1869 the two eldest children, Violet and Cicely, were sent to the West Hall by themselves, 'just like young ladies going to pay a visit', enhanced by the presence of their aunts who were 'young and merry and so kind to us'. Baby Olive was ill, and fearing infection Mrs. Molesworth stayed behind at Tabley Grange with her and Juliet.

But she was too late to prevent Violet from catching the same virulent scarlet fever; and on 6 April she was summoned hastily to the West Hall, only to find her beloved daughter dying or already dead.

'Of all her children I think Violet was perhaps the most dearly loved,' wrote Cicely's daughter long afterwards. 'Even in my youth, thirty or forty years later, my grandmother (if she would speak of it) could remember every little detail of her life and death.'

The whole tragic story of Violet's death is movingly and beautifully told, as if from Cicely's point of view, in 'Good-night, Winny' (*Tell Me a Story*, 1875): 'a narrative of my own children as literal as can be,' wrote Mrs. Molesworth to the critic Edward Salmon in 1887.

Violet, 'A Memory: A.V.G.M.', to whom *Tell Me a Story* is dedicated, was buried at Rostherne, and Mrs. Molesworth, already expecting another child, returned to Tabley Grange, where her eldest son, Richard Walter Stewart, was born four months later, on 13 August— to die at the age of thirteen weeks on 20 November of the same year.

It was perhaps to take her mind off first the one tragedy and then the next that Mrs. Molesworth began her earliest novel, *Lover and Husband*, which was published in 1870 over the pseudonym 'Ennis Graham' which she took from her childhood friend who had died in central Africa. The use of a pen-name was in deference to her father's view that authorship was an unladylike pursuit.

The year after their double tragedy the Molesworths moved from Tabley Grange to the solid, red-brick villa called 'Westfield', spacious and typical of its period, which Charles Stewart had just built for them at High Legh, only a few hundred yards from the West Hall.

Here Mrs. Molesworth continued with her novel-writing, sitting in one of the tall windows looking out towards the main Warrington road; while in the same room her children were being taught by the local school-master. In 'Westfield' two more sons were born, Richard Bevil in 1870, and Lionel Charles in 1873; and there the family might have stayed, had not the link with the West Hall been broken suddenly by Charles Stewart's death in August, 1873, and that of his eldest surviving son a year later. Some legal muddle connected with the two deaths put a sudden and unexpected end to their tenancy of 'Westfield', and the Molesworths may not have been sorry to move to Edinburgh, accompanied by Mrs. Stewart, who had sisters and friends such as Sir Noel Paton the artist, still living there.

This new home was at 25 Royal Terrace, and it was from her window there that Mrs. Molesworth saw the 'two funny little trots' whose story appears in *Carrots*. But at that time her ambition was still to be a novelist, and she had already published three out of the four 'three-deckers' which appeared over the pseudonym of Ennis Graham. Though not great works of literature, these novels are of considerable interest, not least for the light they seem to shed on the vexed question of the break-up of their author's marriage. All suggest that she had gone through a period of great unhappiness, bordering on despair. *Lover and Husband* (1870) and *Not Without Thorns* (1873) refer to the deaths of young children with agonised intensity, while in the latter where the heroine, Eugenia, daughter of a 'Smokytown' business man, falls in love with a young cavalry officer, it seems likely that 'Ennis Graham' was drawing more closely on her own experiences than she herself realised. The main theme of the novel, as of the two earlier ones, is incompatibility of temperament: the hero and heroine are 'totally unsuited to each other in everything except good looks.' We have little positive knowledge about Richard Molesworth, but he seems to have been a straightforward man of action without any deep intellectual interests, while Louisa had a much more complex character.

Her grand-daughter, Mrs. Inglefield, wrote that as a young woman Mrs. Molesworth,

'was perhaps too critical of herself and others, having stronger emotions than she herself realised. The troubles in her marriage and the early deaths of her adored first daughter and her first son undoubtedly soured her for the time being and it was many years before the sweetness came back. I think this accounts for her being so stern a mamma, and so sweet a grand-mother. She was of those natures which resent grief, and only discipline themselves to accept it with great difficulty.'

'So stern' was perhaps a little too emphatic, as Mrs. Inglefield was ready to admit: it was inevitable that Mrs. Molesworth's children should suffer in one way or another from the combined troubles of this period of her life, but the essential tenderness of her nature, revealed in one after another of her children's books, can at no time have been wholly submerged.

She had too much courage and integrity to shrink from self-knowledge. She learned, however painfully, to accept the discipline of suffering, and in the long run to draw from it a new kind of strength, and a deeper understanding of human nature. But in her slow progress towards a greater maturity she was never, for long, led into underestimating the deep significance of the love and happiness she had experienced in childhood and youth. 'She was a very wise person,' said her nephew General Walthall, thinking of her as he knew her towards the end of her life.

Had there been only incompatibility of temperament, and incongruity in their characters, Mrs. Molesworth, like her heroine Eugenia, might well have adapted herself to the situation with her husband. Her outward calm concealed an imaginative and ardent temperament, but there was a strong vein of reasonableness in her make-up—as in so many of her characters, notably those who share her own 'Smokytown' background. So we may assume that it was Richard Molesworth's pathological condition resulting from his Crimean head-wound, which made the marriage overwhelmingly difficult, and ultimately led to separation.

Major Molesworth had retired permanently at the end of 1874, and enforced idleness to one of his active nature must have increased the strain. An Edinburgh friend noted that 'Molesworth had no sense of money .... Mrs. Molesworth probably did not go out much socially in Edinburgh. My impression is that she had a rather anxious time there with Molesworth's extravagance and eccentricity.'

The Molesworths were living at Caen, in 1879, when the marriage finally came to grief, according to a Molesworth cousin, daughter of the 8th Viscount. He went to see Mrs. Molesworth and 'strongly advocated the separation between her and her husband who had become very difficult.' There was a legal separation, but *not* a divorce as has been stated in previous books, and Mrs. Molesworth continued in close friendship with Richard's mother as well as several of his cousins. He lived for a time at Brighton, was made a military 'Knight of Windsor' about 1886, and died in 1900, leaving to his grandsons the memory of a charming and generous eccentric whom they never saw.

Mrs. Molesworth was undoubtedly wise, for the sake of her children, to separate from Richard. But nevertheless they had been deeply in love, and the regret at its outcome is reflected in 'Winter', the last stanza of the poem 'Nature and Love' of which the 'Spring' section was quoted earlier in this chapter:

'Where are the flowers? Where the leaves?
    Where the sweet zephyrs' gentle breath?
Where mellowed fruits and golden sheaves?
    Dead, dead; all icy bound in death!
Is Love too dead? Hence, needless pain!
Love only sleeps to wake again.
Love dead? Ah no, not so with Love;
Love only dies to live above.

Cicely, the last of the four three-volume novels published over the name of Ennis Graham, appeared in 1874. They had created no stir, and were not even popular enough to be reissued as single volumes.

'I have often wondered,' wrote Mrs. Molesworth in 1894, 'how it was that, when it first occurred to me to try my hand at writing, I did not at once choose children's stories. I knew far more about children and child-life than about anything else... Nevertheless, it was not till I had three or four children of my own that I began to *write* for them, and even then, this was owing to the suggestion of a friend with a clearer instinct than I had myself as to what I could do best. To him I shall be for ever grateful. "Better do a small thing *well*," he said, "than a great thing indifferently," when he had been criticising one of the novels that were my first launches into literature.'

The friend who saw where Mrs. Molesworth's real strength lay was Sir Noel Paton, and the first result of his advice was the volume of short tales *Tell Me a Story*, which was published (still as by 'Ennis Graham') by Macmillan, with illustrations by Walter Crane, in 1875.

There was no hesitation on Macmillan's part; he sent for the author, and engaged the leading illustrator of children's books. 'I remember being introduced to Mrs. Molesworth in the late Mr. G. L. Craik's office', wrote Crane in his *Reminiscences* (1907). 'Mr. Craik then acted as reader to the firm, and he arranged with me to supply the illustrations to these very pretty stories.'

'The first stories I published were not so much invention, as narrative,' wrote Mrs. Molesworth, 'the telling, I mean, of real stories—with, of course some little alterations. And even now, though my own stock of childish reminiscences is pretty nearly exhausted, I think I almost always have some ground-work of real fact in every story I write.'

This first book contained 'The Reel Fairies', based on her own childhood; 'Good-night, Winny', the almost exact account of her daughter Violet's death; 'Mary Ann Jolly' one of her mother's stories of childhood in Scotland; two fairy tales; and the little sketch 'Charlie's Disappointment' which may be based on fact.

Carrots: Just a Little Boy the following year presented her own family fairly faithfully (with the addition of the domineering elder boy, Maurice), Captain Desart being modelled to some extent on the irascible Major Molesworth (as his daughter Cicely testifies) and Carrots himself combining the youngest son Lionel, aged four, and Bevil, aged about six. The charming, but a trifle spoilt cousin, Sybil, was Mrs. Molesworth's niece, Agnes Venetia Goring, (daughter of her sister Agnes) who later, as Mrs. Edwin Hohler, published several excellent children's books—rather in her aunt's style.

Mrs. Molesworth was still in Edinburgh when *Carrots* was published, and her first suspicion of its success came just as she was leaving for France and chanced to meet Archibald Constable, the publisher, 'who asked her if she knew that the book was selling extremely well'. A little later, when she was at Pau, the news came through that its reception had far surpassed all expectations, and she was hailed as one of the leading writers for children of the day—a day which still numbered in active practice such writers as Lewis Carroll, George MacDonald, Mrs. Ewing and Charlotte Yonge.

Next year came the book which ensured her fame, and has been a classic from that day to this, *The Cuckoo Clock* (the last to appear as by 'Ennis Graham'). This, her first real imaginative creation, has for basis the cuckoo clock in her children's nursery, while the adventure with the 'Nodding Mandarin' was suggested by the recollection of the Japanese cabinet belonging to her sister which brought back her longings as a little girl to be small enough to explore a miniature one in her own possession.

Mrs. Molesworth was still in Edinburgh when *The Cuckoo Clock* appeared, but the following year she was more or less settled in and near Caen in Northern France, accompanied by her widowed mother, the 'Grandmother Dear' who gave her pet name to the next children's book. The summer of 1878 was spent at the Villa Marie-Jeanne, where another three-volume novel, *Heathercourt Rectory*, was completed; but by October she was living at the Maison du Chanoine in Caen which remained her permanent home for two or three years.

This house, so like the old Wilson 'toon-hoose' at Dunfermline, is generally accepted as the scene in which *The Tapestry Room* (1879) is set—another story of magic overlapping into real life, but still using one at least of her grandmother's traditional tales, 'The Brown Bull of Norrowa'.

Although the children's stories were proving so popular and successful, Mrs. Molesworth seems still to have hankered after her old ambition to be a novelist, and the last of her three-volume efforts, *Miss Bouverie*, appeared in 1880. But when it was reprinted in 1902, with charming illustrations by Lewis Baumer, it was accepted as one of her stories for older girls. Indeed, after 1880 it is difficult to decide which if any of her stories rank as novels, though certainly *Marrying and Giving in Marriage* (1887), *That Girl in Black* (1889), *Leona* (1892), and *The Laurel Walk* (1898) appear to have been intended for adults.

That same year of 1880 saw one of the most unusual of her books, though at its face value merely another of the studies of child-life at which she was becoming such an adept. *A Christmas Child* is the only one of her full-length children's stories with an unhappy ending, in spite of the Victorian liking for pathetic death-bed scenes, wildly overdone in Florence Montgomery's *Misunderstood* (1869)—which Mrs. Molesworth considered definitely unsuitable for children—but brilliantly successful in such miniature pieces as Mrs. Ewing's *The Story of a Short Life* (1882) and Frances E. Crompton's *Friday's Child* (1889).

Mrs. Molesworth's book must be added to the list of successes, even if *A Christmas Child* cannot now be recommended as a story for children. But its special interest lies in the fact that it is an actual biography of a real boy whom she knew, and was written and re-written with infinite care and trouble to achieve accuracy. The original of 'Ted' was Thomas Grindal Hutton (26 Dec. 1862-21 Dec. 1875) whose parents Mrs. Molesworth may have met in Manchester, since Mrs. Hutton's brother (the Uncle in the story who is an expert at 'statistics') was William Stanley Jevons who became Professor of Political Economy at Owens College, Manchester, in 1866. The early part of the book takes place at Plas Eifl, near Nevin in North Wales, but it is the second half, at Ludlow, which is described in loving detail. Mrs. Molesworth stayed there with the Huttons at some time between 1871 and 1875—and once again she found an old Georgian house fronting on a street but with a big walled garden behind, just such a one as is described in *The Cuckoo Clock*. Indeed it is probably more than a coincidence that *The Cuckoo Clock* is dedicated to the memory of Thomas Grindal Hutton, and to his sister Mary Josephine, the 'Narcissa' of *A Christmas Child*.

In a happier vein she immortalised her own youngest child Lionel in *The Adventures of Herr Baby* on a trip to the south of France; and presented her daughter Juliet as the heroine of *Hoodie*, a brilliant story which seems to have run away with her so that her sense of artistic achievement blinded her to the effect the story might have on the unfortunate Juliet, whose daughter writes:

'My poor mother had tantrums, and *Hoodie* was rather written about her, and she was told this and

43

suffered agonies thinking everyone would know, when it was published.'

It must certainly have been disconcerting to be a child related to Mrs. Molesworth and find oneself suddenly in a story, only thinly disguised: 'My aunt made use of any little stories she heard,' wrote Helen Delves Walthall, her niece and god-daughter: 'In fact we, her own children, and her other nephews and nieces, appear in several.'

Mrs. Molesworth's fame and popularity were growing fast, and Swinburne wrote of her work early in 1884:

'It seems to me not at all easier to draw a life-like child than to draw a life-like man or woman . . . Since the death of George Eliot, there is none left whose touch is so exquisite and masterly, whose love is so thoroughly according to knowledge, whose bright and sweet invention is so fruitful, so truthful or so delightful as Mrs. Molesworth's. Any chapter of *The Cuckoo Clock* or the enchanting *Adventures of Herr Baby* is worth a shoal of the very best novels dealing with the characters and fortunes of mere adults.'

Meanwhile Mrs. Molesworth was living quietly in France with her children and her mother. In the earlier years their centre was the Maison du Chanoine at Caen, varied by summers at villas rented in the country, such as La Maison Rose at Benières. Later she made her headquarters in Paris, taking *appartements* in the Avenue Kleber (the rooms described in *Two*

44

Little Waifs, 1883) and at Avenue Jena 55 (probably those of 'Grandmother Dear's Old Watch'—*Aunt Judy's Magazine*, 1884; collected in *A Christmas Posy*, 1888.)

Mrs. Molesworth also spent several fairly long periods in Germany, sometimes leaving two or three of her children with their grandmother in Paris. Coburg was her centre for a time, and on one occasion at least she made expeditions through Thuringen, where something resembling the strange experience in 'Unexplained' (*Macmillan's Magazine*, May, 1885; collected in *Four Ghost Stories*, 1888) may have befallen her: the story is set so precisely in 1879, and Nora and Reggie agree in age and description with Olive and Bevil.

Several of her children's stories are set in Thuringen, the most notable being the fantasy, *Christmas Tree Land* (1884), and the amusing short tale of 'The Blue Dwarfs' (*Aunt Judy's Magazine*, Feb. 1882; collected in *A Christmas Posy*, 1888) in which Olive appears by name and Bevil is now 'Rex'.

Mrs. Stewart died in the summer of 1883, and with Bevil now approaching public school age, Mrs. Molesworth decided that she must return permanently to England. She spent the late summer at Hohwald in the Vosges, where her husband's cousin Gwen Molesworth came to join the party, and recollected her 'sitting on a log, with us all around her, telling us ghost stories'. Then she came back to London in the autumn, arriving perhaps on just such a day of gloom and fog as she describes as greeting a similar home-coming in *Blanche* (1894), and settled at 85, Lexham Gardens.

This house depressed her, and in 1890 she removed

thankfully to 19 Sumner Place, just off Onslow Square (the Square which figures in several of her stories, such as *The Wood-pigeons and Mary*, 1901, and in Olive's one book, *The Trio in the Square*, 1898) where she remained for ten years, before her final move to a flat at 155, Sloane Street, where she lived until her death twenty-two years later.

In these London houses Mrs. Molesworth was visited by many well-known people, ranging from Walter Pater, Edwin Arnold and Aubrey de Vere, to Kipling, just arrived from India, or Swinburne and Watts-Dunton—'I thought he never left Putney', wrote Grant Duff, 'but now I remember, he does sometimes, in order to lunch with his dear friend Louisa Molesworth, who made the *Cuckoo Clock* chime.'

A good picture of her at this time is given by Gwen Molesworth (Mrs. Dyson-Laurie):

'Mrs. Molesworth was very attractive looking, tall and dignified, with a quiet calm manner. One could not imagine her romping on the floor with small children. Her manner was distant and one worshipped from afar. She adored her girls, Mrs. Prinsep (Cicely) was like a sister to her, and later on Olive and she were absolutely one and could not bear to be separated from each other. Her daughters did the housekeeping and she sat down regularly to write every morning after breakfast ... Her humour was quiet, but appreciative, and I cannot remember her laughing very heartily ... She did not like being disturbed at all times, and some people gave up calling at Sloane Street because they said it was very difficult to get in ... She was very methodical and exact, budgeting carefully all her expenses, otherwise I do not think they could have lived in the style they did. She liked good clothes and was always well turned out, fresh and up to date ... She had a very young figure, and as her hair was never grey she did not look her years.'

Although London was her home from 1884 onwards, Mrs. Molesworth would frequently take a house in the country during the summer. Thus they were at St. Davids in South Wales in 1885, where Walter Crane and his children were also spending the summer, and another year she took a house near Penmaenmawr in North Wales for six months—making use of her Welsh experiences in *The Old Pincushion* (as *Aunt Clotilda's Guests* in *Little Folks*, July-Dec. 1887; in book form, 1889) and to a less extent in one of the best of her magical stories, *The Children of the Castle* (1890). She also spent several holidays with her sister Caroline Delves Walthall at Pen-y-Bont, St. Asaph, while one summer she took a house called 'Old Way' at Paignton in Devon. She was often a guest at country houses: a visit to Ashfield House, West Malvern in 1893 may have given her the idea for 'Windy Gap' in *My New Home* the following year, and as her daughters married (Cicely to James Charles Prinsep in 1893, and Juliet to Julian Grant-Duff Ainslee in 1898) she also spent holidays at their homes.

Richard Bevil, the eldest surviving son, did not marry and departed to South America in 1889 whence

47

he sent back one short story, 'A Ghost of the Pampas', which was published in *The Newberry House Magazine* for April, 1893, and reprinted by Mrs. Molesworth in her collection of adult stories, *The Wrong Envelope*, in 1906. Bevil did not return to England, but died on his ranch in Patagonia in 1898.

The youngest son, Lionel Charles, went up to University College, Oxford, but left without taking a degree, to get married in 1896 and become a land agent at Cirencester. In 1901 Mrs. Molesworth was able to dedicate *My Pretty and her Little Brother Too* to 'my first grandson, Roger Bevil Molesworth'; and in 1909 one of her last books, *The February Boys*, described the adventures of Carrot's children, at the time when 'Rolf' shows signs of becoming jealous of the baby brother born almost on his birthday—just as Lionel's second son was, in February, 1907.

And as she had once read her stories to her own children (but only after placing the manuscript between the pages of a book so that she could pretend that it was a published work by someone else that she was reading—and so obtain an unbiased judgement), Mrs. Molesworth was able to try out her last stories on her grandchildren. The Hon. Mrs. Grant Bruce (Juliet's daughter), looking back to the early years of the century in a letter written to Ruth Robertson in 1952, gives a charming picture of the old lady who was still so young at heart and so fresh in invention:

'An annual event was the summer visit from my grandmother. She must have come about June each year. She always brought the MS. of the book or short story she was writing at the time. All her books were in her clear, legible writing with hardly an erasure, and they went to the printers like this . . . We used to sit round her in a circle on the lawn. Sometimes our cousins, children of her elder daughter (Cicely), would be staying and we all loved to be the first to hear a story no one else knew about. She read in a soft voice full of expression which made it all alive. Sometimes she was still in process of writing and would ask our advice, and quite often took our suggestions. I remember this particularly in a book of short stories called *Fairies Afield* (her last book, published in 1911). I was rather sorry she had dedicated *Fairies—of Sorts* (1908) to her nine Grandchildren. I much preferred the stories in *Fairies Afield*, perhaps because I had had more to do with their writing, and had asked her to write one about a Weather House ('The Weather Maiden'; reprinted in *Fairy Stories*, 1957). But most of us had sat round her listening to the earlier book, so she had dedicated that one to us.

'I think really, to sum up, we regarded my grandmother with a sort of awed interest, but she didn't touch our lives nearly, though we felt quite proud to have our opinions asked and used, and to have her as a relation.'

Mary Louisa Molesworth was loved and admired by many. The daughter of one of her closest friends, Miss Julia Du Cane, recollected her as 'a woman of very considerable charm of a quiet, gentle and almost deprecatory kind. She had a very quiet soft voice which I personally found very attractive.' Yet there was an element of reserve in her nature which could be a little intimidating. Lady Goring's daughter wrote, 'I was very fond of Great-aunt Louisa, but she was one of the people we always had to be on our best behaviour with,' and her grandson Mr. H. D. Molesworth, who saw her only very rarely, felt ill-at-ease and constrained in her company. It is fairest, perhaps, to let a final comment on her character come from Mrs. Inglefield, the granddaughter who lived near her in London for many years and saw her almost daily.

'My grandmother was not an easy person to know. She was very reserved, not at all gushing. She was, I believe, a strict even a stern mamma—but a more dearly loved grandmother never lived.'

Mrs. Molesworth gave up writing after *Fairies Afield* in 1911, probably considering this to be her hundredth book—two short stories re-issued in a tiny volume by Ernest Nister in 1903 may well have appeared without her knowledge.

The last ten years of her life were passed quietly at 155 Sloane Street, only interrupted by the first World War in which she occupied herself in work for the wounded, and she died quietly of heart failure on 20 July, 1921, and was buried in Brompton Cemetery.

IV. The Writer in her Setting

When Mrs. Molesworth began to write for children in 1875, the awakening to the Golden Age of children's books ushered in by *Alice's Adventures in Wonderland* was but ten years old. The new freedom inaugurated by Lewis Carroll had spread fast, but was so far to be found chiefly in tales of fantasy and the imagination—the excuse deemed needful by the Olympians for the sudden break away to joyful high spirits and the irresponsible sunshine of the real Child World out of the gloom of instruction and decorum which had been shed over the first half of the century.

While *Alice* had found followers, strivers after the inimitable, of whom Jean Ingelow and Tom Hood were the best with *Mopsa the Fairy* (1869) and *Pesetilla's Posy* (1870), George MacDonald had but brushed past Wonderland with 'The Light Princess' in his *Dealing with the Fairies* (1867) to find a truer and deeper Fairyland of the soul in *The Princess and the Goblin* (1872), and to knock on the fairy wicket that divides actual from spiritual experience in *At the Back of the North Wind* (1871). The fairy tale built on the traditional models had felt a new breath of immortality in the best of MacDonald's short stories, in one or two of Mary de Morgan's first volume of tales, collected as *On a Pincushion* (1877), and in Mrs. Ewing's *Old Fashioned Fairy Tales*, which were appearing in *Aunt Judy's Magazine* (though not collected until 1882).

The conception of the child as a real and interesting personality, living and dreaming in a world of its own, and not always conscious of the struggle into adulthood, which was to find complete expression in *The Golden Age* and *Dream Days* at the end of the century, was triumphing fast over the idea of the child as a miniature and inferior adult—the incomplete person to be trained into manhood almost like a dog, broken to bear the burdens of life as a horse is broken to docility and service. The poems of Elizabeth Ann Hart (with a small number by her sister Menella Smedley in the first two volumes) published in 1868 and 1869 as *Poems written for a Child, Child-World* and *Child-Nature*—books from which Mrs. Molesworth quoted more frequently than those of any other writer—were a brilliant and undeservedly forgotten foretaste of the understanding of childhood which was so near.

Mrs. Hart's first story for children, *The Runaway* (1872) was only matched by Mrs. Ewing's *A Flat Iron for a Farthing* published the same year, and *Lob Lie-by-the-fire* of two years later, and surpassed by her greatest child-novels, *Six to Sixteen* (1875) and *Jan of the Windmill* (1876). Although 1875 also saw Mrs. Craik's beautiful fairy allegory *The Little Lame Prince* and George MacDonald's greatest book, *The Princess and Curdie*, did not appear until 1883, the trend towards realism was already strong, and grew during the next decade until Mrs. E. M. Field could write in 1889 that 'the fairy-tale seems to have given way entirely in popularity to the child's story of real life, the novel of childhood, in which no effort is spared to make children appear as they are'.

In spite of her occasional departure into the realms

of fantasy, Mrs. Molesworth was the most powerful influence in this trend, and Edward Salmon wrote in 1887 that her 'great charm is her realism—realism, that is, in the purest and highest sense', while substantiating his claim that:

'Mrs. Molesworth is, in my opinion, considering the quality and quantity of her labours, the best story-teller for children England has yet known.'

The influence which she exerted towards 'realism' was to a large extent due to her own particular gifts, her understanding of children and of the child's out-look and thoughts—the extremely vivid memory of her own child-mind and the sheer strength of her imagin-ation—the outward signs of the peculiar touch of genius which was undoubtedly hers: the 'knack' which was all she would ever admit to.

Her own account of how she wrote her children's stories brings us a little nearer to an understanding of her peculiar excellence. At first there was the 'inspir-ation', though she did not call it this:

'As to "what puts a story into my head", you would be amused if I could tell you what very tiny things are often responsible for that', she wrote in her *Little Folks* article in 1894. 'The look of a garden at a certain hour of the day, the sound of rustling leaves in the wind, a pretty name, some far-away remembrance of my own childhood, which for years and years I had forgotten— all these things and a host of others, too small and

53

almost too indescribable to explain, have suggested my stories.'

Then came the fairly long period of gestation described in 'On the Art of Writing Fiction for Children', first published in L.T. Meade's magazine *Atalanta* in May, 1893:

'The great thing is to make the aquaintance of your characters, and get to know them as well and intimately as you possibly can . . . I generally begin by finding names for all my personages. I marshal them before me and call the roll, to which each answers in turn, and then I feel I have my "troupe" complete, and I proceed to take them more in detail. I live with them as much as I can, often for weeks, before I have done more than write down their names. I listen to what they talk about to each other in their own homes, not with the intention of writing it down, but by way of, as I said, getting to know them well. And by degrees I feel them becoming very real. I can say to myself sometimes, when sitting idly doing nothing in particular, "Now whom shall I go to see for a little—the So-and-So's, or little somebody?"—whatever the names may be that I have given; and so day by day I seem to be more in their lives, more able to tell how, in certain circumstances, my characters would comport themselves. And by degrees these circumstances stretch themselves out and take vague shape . . . I seldom care to look far ahead, though at the same time a certain grasp of the whole situation is, and has been, I think, there from the first. It never seems to

me that my characters come into existence, like phant-
oms, merely for the time I want them. Rather do I feel
that I am selecting certain incidents out of real lives . . .
I always feel as if somewhere the children I have
learnt to love are living, growing into men and women
like my own real sons and daughters. I always feel
as if there were ever so much more to hear about
them.'

This careful thought was followed by careful writing
—in the mechanical sense, in that she made a rule of
never re-writing: 'I write at once as I intend the words
to stand,' she said, feeling that it added vigour and
freshness to the style, and made for far more careful
thought and construction—but also, and more signific-
antly, in the selection and arrangement of the plot and
incidents.

'The whole position is strangely complicated,' she
wrote in 'Story-Writing' in *The Monthly Packet* (1894).
'You have to be yourself, with your experience, your
knowledge of good and alas! of evil too; and at the same
time you must be the child, or at least in the child's
place, and that, again, without any *apparent* stepping
down. The very writing that appeals to its own feelings
and sympathies, that makes the boy or girl conscious of
being "understood", should have a reserve of something
more—something higher and yet deeper. While you
amuse and interest, you should all the time be *lifting*;
yet, above all, without preaching. Children's stories
should be like the pure bracing air of some mountain

height—unconsciously strengthening towards all good, while assimilated with no realised effort.'

The abiding sense of duty which runs through the stories is certainly one of the most notable characteristics to the adult reader—and, except in very few and usually early cases, the complete absence of any direct moral teaching. Mrs. Molesworth very literally 'built on the Rock', and to a considerable extent it is this fact which gives so much of the deep interest and durability to her books. The modern child may be led by her into a strange world where mysterious people like nurses and servants play an important part, and the very children wear period costume: but the basic values are the same and are accepted unquestioningly. The assurance and the reality are there and are recognised instinctively, and the reader accepts the strangeness immediately and finds in it an actual heightening of the enjoyment. The rules of the game may be quaint though interesting, and easy to learn; but there is nothing unnatural about the game itself. The problems of Mrs. Molesworth's children may be coloured by their period, but the mental conflict behind them is common to us all.

This deep reality, both without and within, makes Mrs. Molesworth one of the relatively few writers for children who, at their best, can be equally satisfying to the adult. On one level the problems and anxieties of Carrots or Hoodie or Geraldine bring back to us vividly the recollection of the days when our outlook and reaction were just as theirs; at supreme moments their struggles and their doubts mirror with exceptional clarity our own predicaments, seen the more clearly in the unusual microscopic field. Finally, the absolute acceptance and the loving care in presentation of a past age give us a startlingly real and convincing picture: to know what the child-life of our Victorian grandparents and great-grandparents was really like we have but to turn to Mrs. Molesworth for the full, true and accurate picture. We may begin in the nursery with *Carrots*, and *Mary*, and so pass by way of *Little Miss Peggy* and *Hermy* into the school-room with *Little Mother Bunch* and *The Oriel Window*, away on holiday with *The Old Pincushion*, to the country with *Nurse Heatherdale's Story* and *Sheila's Mystery*, to London with *My New Home* or to the seaside with *The Rectory Children*, to Paris with *Two Little Waifs* (or with *French Life in Letters*, Mrs. Molesworth's one 'lesson-book', written in admirable French) or to Germany with *The Little Guest*, and by way of *The Carved Lions* out of the home through the more unusual boarding-school; and finally into older girlhood and young-womanhood in a score of clever, if less noteworthy novels for girls, from *Blanche* and *Meg Langholme* to *The Red Grange* and *Miss Bouverie*.

Mrs. Molesworth has been accused of snobbery—though it is a failing which she attacks almost violently in several of her books. 'She would be a common-minded, inferior woman in *any* class,' says one of her characters of a titled snob. 'I believe that is the truth of it all: there are refined and charming natures to be found in every class, and there are the opposite.' Mrs.

57

Molesworth certainly accepts without question the class system of her day—'Ancient, effortless, ordered'—and many of her girl-novels turn on small points of propriety and etiquette magnified into such importance that they can be read now only as curiosities. But, accepting this, she could write with complete sympathy and understanding of all walks of life, more convincingly even than her contemporary Mrs. Hodgson Burnett; and she had no mercy on the upper class child who looks down upon or patronises the child from a lower social order. Nor does she attempt to segregate them, nor suggest that one is 'better' than the other: she might have quoted 'all men are equal in the sight of God', while adding provided they do their duty 'in that station of life into which it has pleased God to call them'. In her beautiful allegorical fantasy *The Children of the Castle* it is Winfried the fisherboy who has risen highest from the Christian point of view, and Bertrand the nephew of the lord of the Castle who is only at the bottom of the ladder; and *Four Winds Farm* is concerned with the spiritual journey of Gratian the farmer's son. In the same way, the bookseller's daughter becomes the friend and exemplar of *The Rectory Children*; the objectionable Geoff in *Great Uncle Hoot-Toot* is brought to his senses by being made a farm-hand (just as Hervey Cheyne was made a fisherman a few years later in Kipling's *Captains Courageous*), and jealous Sheila in *Sheila's Mystery* benefits also by the temporary belief that she is only a farmer's daughter. Even the very poor, dwelling in the back-streets of Manchester or Liverpool, are described with realism and sympathy in *Little Miss Peggy* (drawn from her actual experiences as a child in Rusholme Road) and *Farthings*, though Mrs. Molesworth is always careful to avoid the morbidity of Brenda and Hesba Stretton.

Perhaps the book which gives the clearest picture of Mrs. Molesworth's world in perfect action is *Nurse Heatherdale's Story* (1891) which presents a cross-section of life from the cottage to the castle as seen by the old nurse who follows the fortunes of an impoverished county family through a series of enthralling adventures which make it particularly acceptable to the child reader.

In books like this and *Two Little Waifs*, and best of all in *The Carved Lions*, Mrs. Molesworth may fairly be described as the Jane Austen of the nursery. Although her books are to Jane Austen's as the miniature is to the great painting, they are as nearly perfect in their small kind as the great novelist's are in hers. Like *Pride and Prejudice* they are 'period' without being dated; they appeal to the heart as well as to the intellect; they remain in the memory and enrich the experience; they not only played an important part in our literature, but deserve an abiding place on our shelves to be read and re-read by young and old.

Mrs. Molesworth, wrote *The Times* obituarist, 'has a way with her, a fragrance of thought which children instinctively recognize, and adults consciously enjoy.' That fragrance is apparent in so many of her stories, and the skill of presentation which makes the adventures of her children so absorbing, that it is hard to select the best out of quite half of her hundred and one books which have some claims to be remembered.

Undoubtedly *The Carved Lions* (1895) wins by a short head among her stories of real life, which are the books that appeal most strongly to the adult as well as to the child. The story of Geraldine's experiences as she goes from the quiet happiness of her home in 'the dull house in the dull street' in Manchester to the unexpected trials and tribulations of boarding-school, until the end of her endurance is reached and she runs away to seek shelter in the shop where the Carved Lions stand, and wakes after a dream that is almost real to find herself among new friends, is told with a most delicate and sensitive touch, with the highest artistic finish and restraint. Of all her stories it is the most convincing, the most perfect example of observation, experience and imagination blended into a living and harmonious whole by the gentle and compelling touch of genius which was hers.

Only a little less compelling are the adventures of Gladys and Roger, the *Two Little Waifs* (1883) lost and found in Paris, children much younger than Geraldine and her brother, yet almost as perfectly understood and presented from within.

Invention and 'make-believe' are not as obvious characteristics of Mrs. Molesworth's children as they are of E. Nesbit's. But she was none the less aware of their importance and prevalence in the child world. The early story 'Six Poor Little Princesses' (collected in *A Christmas Posy*, 1888, and reprinted in *Tales of Make-Believe* in Dent's Children's Illustrated Classics in 1960) is an admirable example of this; but no longer story turns to any great extent on it until the amusing *Peterkin* (1902), the gayest of all Mrs. Molesworth's books, which perhaps shows a little influence from the outbreak into a more carefree world begun by Kenneth Grahame and exploited in *The Treasure Seekers*.

This new breath of exhilarating wind also makes *The House that Grew* (1900) one of the outstanding stories, and introduces some of Mrs. Molesworth's least self-conscious children in an unusually dashing atmosphere of holiday adventure. As her last full-length book, however, she produced in *The Story of a Year* (1910) a beautiful study of another lonely child in a thinly disguised mid-Victorian Manchester, to make a fit pendant to *The Carved Lions*.

In spite of the supreme excellencies of these stories, Mrs. Molesworth is, however, best known as the author of *The Cuckoo Clock*, a book which perhaps gets more completely into the child-mind than any of the others, and is more wholly acceptable to the child, though less so to the adult. Although George MacDonald may have led the way out of the well-known house through the unexpected doorway into the fourth dimension, Mrs. Molesworth brought this new kingdom far nearer to the average child, even if she did not penetrate so deeply into these misty regions of the soul.

The Cuckoo Clock has been welcomed in the New World as well as the Old. One American child, when asked what book she loved best when she was little, named this one, and knew its opening words by heart.

'Everything in the book was old and mysterious,' she said, 'except the little girl and the cuckoo.'*

'Once upon a time in an old town, in an old street, there stood a very old house. Such a house as you could hardly find nowadays, however you searched, for it belonged to a gone-by time—a time now quite passed away.

'It stood in a street, but yet it was not like a town house, for though the front opened right on to the pavement the back windows looked out upon a beautiful, quaintly terraced garden with old trees growing so thick and close together that in summer it was like living on the edge of a forest to be near them; and indeed even in winter the web of their interlaced branches hid all clear view behind.

'Time indeed seemed to stand still in and all about the old house. . . .'

Despite the Cranford-like setting in the old house of her great-aunts, Griselda is the eternal and ubiquitous child in search of an ordinary Fairyland. The cuckoo comes down from the clock and leads her up to his little house in it, or to the palace of the Nodding Mandarins, just as Dudu the Raven leads the children out of *The Tapestry Room*, more naturally and more according to a child's dream-fancies than their descendant the Psammead and the Phoenix were to lead E. Nesbit's

Choosing books for Children, May Lamberton Becker. (1937). *The Cuckoo Clock* and *The Tapestry Room* have also been popular in New Zealand.

children across the borders of reality thirty years later.

Griselda entertained in the Cuckoo's little room in the clock, or dressed and feasted by the butterflies, show Mrs. Molesworth's complete ability to think or remember a child's thoughts. But there are greater depths to *The Cuckoo Clock*, and we glimpse with Griselda that real Fairyland beyond any region of fancy to which the Cuckoo can lead her.

This touch of mysticism, this longing for the unseen —or for the true reality—is not often apparent in Mrs. Molesworth's stories, though it can usually be felt in the background, just as Fulvia in *The Story of a Year* feels that Miss Guise's house is *'scented* with niceness'.

Her sense of the unseen could lead Mrs. Molesworth into her liking for ghost stories, of which she wrote almost a dozen for adults, collected in *Four Ghost Stories*, (1888) and *Uncanny Tales* (1896). But her real height in this field was attained with *Four Winds Farm* in 1886 and *The Children of the Castle* (1890), books which reach out after the infinite in a way which only George MacDonald had attempted, and which was perhaps not achieved again until C. S. Lewis began to write of Narnia in 1950.

While *Four Winds Farm* is the better story, *The Children of the Castle* achieves greater heights of vision and revelation, and the indefinable touch of the numinous which makes of it a deep and lasting experience. Yet at its face value it is an exciting story of Ruby and Mavis who live in the old castle by the seashore, who meet Winfried the fisherboy about whom clings a touch of mystery, of how their rough and unkind spoilt cousin

Bertrand plays one trick too many—and the effect on all four of them of the magic of the strange Princess Forget-me-not, which includes a visit to Forget-me-not-Land, which at first sight seems to be in the same world as Griselda's Butterfly Land.

Although she failed to reach such heights again in *The Wood-pigeons and Mary* (1901) or *The Ruby Ring* (1904), Mrs. Molesworth did not ever lose her touch of magic. Superb fairy tales, outwardly in the old folklore tradition, crop up from time to time as 'inset-stories' in such books as *Christmas-Tree Land* (1884), *The Magic Nuts* (1898) and *The Little Guest* (1907). But she wrote also two excellent collections of fairy stories, *An Enchanted Garden* (1892) and her last book, *Fairies Afield* (1911), which must rank among her most important and lasting works.

v. 'Where *are* that Cuckoo?'

Just as one can know Mrs. Molesworth as intimately as a personal friend through her books, and yet be left with very few definite facts about her life after reading them all, so it is almost impossible to isolate or describe what it is in her writings that seems to stamp them with the touch of genius that sets them above most of those of her contemporaries and ensures some at least of immortality.

It seems at first sight easy to point out how much better several other writers are than Mrs. Molesworth. Edith Nesbit wrote more obviously exciting stories; on the face of it she could produce greater suspense; she had a more obvious sense of humour; she raced through her stories, leaping from invention to invention with a breath-taking delight in the joy of movement— and we rush along with her and gladly surrender to the enchantment. E. Nesbit in her books seems a child who has never grown up: she writes just what we would write as children—if only we knew how. She knows all there is to be known about the visible aspects of childhood; but of what lies beneath the surface she does not tell. She can see to a little distance: Oswald is firmly rooted. But when she pries deeper, the waters become thick and cloying as in the story of the soldier's tombstone, and in much of *The Railway Children*.

At first glance Mrs. Molesworth seldom has much of a story to tell; her children seem a little too sedate and well-behaved—they play, but they never appear to romp; they dirty their hands, but they seldom tear their clothes. Their adventures are not particularly exciting—even when the *Two Little Waifs* get lost in Paris, or the Treluans of *Nurse Heatherdale's Story* find hidden treasure—and Dudu or the Cuckoo bring no magic comparable in its outward effects to the gifts of the Psammead.

Critics in her own day tried to pin-point Mrs. Molesworth's touch of genius: 'She has a way with her, a fragrance of thought', says one; 'Mrs. Molesworth's great charm is her realism,' says another—and then hastens to qualify the realism as 'in the purest and highest sense'; Swinburne simply generalises with 'exquisite and masterly' touch, 'bright and sweet invention', love 'so thoroughly according to knowledge'. They were all right in a certain sense: we should not, ideally, have to define these things: modern analytical criticism is a new and monstrous growth that would dissect the rose in search of its scent.

But since we must probe, must index the allegory and strive to define what seems so obvious to our subconsious appreciation as we read, it seems that realism is indeed the keynote in Mrs. Molesworth's symphony. Her recollections of her own childhood were so clear that she could recapture something of what goes on in a child's mind; she could, perhaps, see into the minds of children with whom she came in contact—even though there were lapses where her own children were concerned, and she failed to set Juliet's reactions against the salutary lesson which *Hoodie* should so obviously have taught her.

Overwhelmingly in her best stories (and to some extent in everything that she wrote for children) Mrs.

Molesworth demonstrates this almost uncanny power of sharing the child's experience. Shorn of the jargon and the dubious interpretations, she is a superb psychologist without any conscious intentions: she described how she lived with and got to know her fictional families —her gift is to make us members of those families while we read. Once this is done, the slight story becomes of overwhelming importance: Geraldines's experiences, her hopes, disappointments, disillusionments and despair at Green Bank were so utterly and soul-searingly vital to her at the time that they affected her subconscious to the extent of causing the healing dream which perhaps saved her sanity as she slept by the Carved Lions. In this story, perhaps, more firmly than in any of her others, the magic is complete: at any age the reader is wafted by it into the story, is made one with Geraldine—and at once the simple little plot becomes utterly absorbing and a living part of one's own experience.

Again and again this experience comes to the reader of Mrs. Molesworth's stories. Perhaps not always so compellingly; perhaps more compellingly in one story rather than another to different readers. Here criticism falls down, as it so often does with the great works of romance, and sometimes with the acknowledged masterpieces of humour. But the keynote of literary metempsychosis, of a realism which has the power of sharing fictional experience, seems to be sufficiently general to pass as an interpretation of Mrs. Molesworth's claim to genius.

The depth of shared experience rarely requires the

introduction of actual magic, and perhaps it was a tacit admission of defeat which caused Mrs. Molesworth to summon supernatural powers to her aid in *Four Winds Farm* and *The Children of the Castle*. In the first of these she certainly had a personal experience to deal with which touched a deep chord that seemed beyond rational explanation. Her earliest memory was of 'a storm of wind' which:

'left a stange and awe-inspiring impression upon me— the realization of an actual power I had not till then known of, for it lifted me off my feet. I felt that it was something I could not resist, though it was formless and invisible. I was terrified, but far more astounded. I never forgot it; I never shall forget it.'

This may suggest that Mrs. Molesworth was an emotional writer: she was certainly an intuitive one, and her intuition suffered frequently from the super- imposed form of her stories, which were usually serial- ised in six monthly parts in such periodicals as *Little Folks*. Again and again a slow start has risen gradually towards a superb climax, when the last number has suddenly loomed in front of her, and an abrupt ending left us asking desperately for more. This may explain why all her best books are among those written for annual publication by Macmillan without previous serialisation. They are seldom any longer than the serial stories but, once she had got into her stride by about 1883, they are usually perfectly constructed wholes, neither desperately padded like *Carrots*, nor two stories dovetailed together like the serialised *Hermy*, nor woefully truncated like *Little Mother Bunch*.

The kind of artistry which makes the perfect whole of *Two Little Waifs* and *Nurse Heatherdale's Story*, *The Carved Lions* and *Peterkin* cannot be illustrated by description or quotation, any more than the simple style and slow unfolding of character, the setting of the scene and the tiny touches which woo the reader gently into the story until the surrender of personality becomes complete. Separate excellencies, like the vivid descriptions, notably of Griselda's dress in *The Cuckoo Clock* (quoted and analysed admirably by Marghanita Laski in her *Mrs. Ewing, Mrs. Molesworth and Mrs. Hodgson Burnett*), mean less in themselves than as part of the *mise en scène*. The place-backgrounds, again, are developed so subtly throughout the books in which they are of importance that no quotation can illustrate them. One does not pause to think what an effect the rain and the grey streets and the lack of green life has on *The Carved Lions*, any more than one consciously chalks up a good mark for the first 'little breakfast' which accentuates the devastatingly alien nature of the predicament of Gladys and Roger, the *Two Little Waifs* in Paris, more vitally than any statement or description could have done.

One may end by underlining the fact that Mrs. Molesworth's remarkable achievement in capturing the sensations and the little things of childhood is accomplished against an uncompromisingly Victorian setting. Mere period pieces do not and could not appeal to children, and for this reason superficially competent writers among her contemporaries like L. T. Meade and Evelyn Everett Green are forgotten save by antiquarians and students of literature. But even without the inspired nonsense of Lewis Carroll, the compelling allegory of George MacDonald or the exuberant make-believe and the infectious gaiety of E. Nesbit, Mrs. Molesworth has never lost her hold. She may, like Jane Austen or Mrs. Gaskell among adults, appeal only to a relative minority, but appeal she does and that strongly. Although her popularity touched low water in the two decades after her death, she has never been quite out of print, and her books have been coming back slowly but surely during the last twenty years.

The Cuckoo Clock was one of the first four titles to be printed by Puffin Story Books in 1941; Macmillan's offer it with illustrations by Walter Crane or by C. E. Brock, and Dent's Illustrated Children's Classics included it in 1954 with superb pictures by Ernest Shepard. *The Carved Lions* returned in 1947 in Marghanita Laski's omnibus volume of *Victorian Tales for Girls*, and 1960 saw an excellent new edition of the story from the Faith Press. *Carrots* and *The Tapestry Room* are available with the old Crane illustrations, or the latter with a new frontispiece to accompany *The Ruby Ring* and a selection of Mrs. Molesworth's *Fairy Stories* over the imprint of the Harvill Press, while several others, including *Christmas Tree Land, Four Winds Farm, The Children of the Castle* and *Nurse Heatherdale's Story*, are on lists of 'forthcoming books'. She is now no longer neglected by anthologists, and half a dozen of her

70

books have been serialised by the B.B.C., some like *The Carved Lions*, more than once.

We may surely say now, without the wishful thinking of the enthusiast, that Mrs. Molesworth's place in our literature is certain, and her appeal to young readers is both proven and assured.

A MRS MOLESWORTH BOOK LIST

There is no published Bibliography of Mrs Molesworth's works. Lists, varying in accuracy and completeness appear in Roger Lancelyn Green's *Tellers of Tales* (1946; Revised edition 1953) and in Marghanita Laski's *Mrs. Ewing, Mrs. Molesworth and Mrs. Hodgson Burnett* (1950). Under these circumstances it has seemed worth giving here as full and accurate a list as possible—including for the sake of completeness her half-dozen novels and four volumes of short stories intended primarily for adults.

In the main section titles are given in Capitals, publishers in lower case and illustrators in *italic*. Where a date appears by itself in square brackets it is not given in the book; where a date in brackets accompanies an unbracketed date, the first may be taken as correct, though the second is that printed in the book. Full entries in square brackets are of later editions, which are included under the main entry for each book.

I. BOOKS BY MRS MOLESWORTH

LOVER AND HUSBAND. 3 vols. Skeet.   1870

SHE WAS YOUNG AND HE WAS OLD. 3 vols. Tinsley.   1872

NOT WITHOUT THORNS. 3 vols. Tinsley.   1873

CICELY: A STORY OF THREE YEARS. 3 vols. Tinsley.   1874

TELL ME A STORY. Macmillan. *Walter Crane.*   1875

CARROTS: JUST A LITTLE BOY. Macmillan. *Walter Crane.*   1876

THE CUCKOO CLOCK. Macmillan. *Walter Crane.* [Macmillan. *C. E. Brock.* (*c.* 1920); Puffin Story Books. 1941; Ingram. *Sylvia Green.* 1948; Dent. *Ernest H. Shepard.* 1954].   1877

HATHERCOURT RECTORY. 3 vols. Hurst and Blackett.   1878

GRANDMOTHER DEAR: A BOOK FOR BOYS AND GIRLS. Macmillan. *Walter Crane.*   1878

THE TAPESTRY ROOM: A CHILD'S ROMANCE. Macmillan. *Walter Crane.* [Harvill Press. *Astrid Walford.* 1957].

MISS BOUVERIE. 3 vols. Hurst and Blackett. [Chambers. *Lewis Baumer.* 1902].   1880

A CHRISTMAS CHILD: A SKETCH OF BOY-LIFE. Macmillan. *Walter Crane.*   1880

HERMY: THE STORY OF A LITTLE GIRL. Rout-
ledge. *Mary Ellen Edwards*. [Chambers. *Lewis Baumer.*
1898]. 1881
THE ADVENTURES OF HERR BABY. Macmillan.
Walter Crane. 1881
HOODIE. Routledge. *Mary Ellen Edwards.*
[Chambers. *Lewis Baumer.* 1897]. [1881] 1882
SUMMER STORIES FOR BOYS AND GIRLS. Mac-
millan. 1882
ROSY. Macmillan. *Walter Crane*. 1882
THE BOYS AND I: A CHILD'S STORY FOR CHILD-
REN. Routledge. *Mary Ellen Edwards*. [1882] 1883
TWO LITTLE WAIFS. Macmillan. *Walter Crane*. 1883
LETTICE. Society for Promoting Christian Knowledge.
Frank Dadd. [1884]
THE LITTLE OLD PORTRAIT. S.P.C.K. *W. Gunston.*
[as EDMÉE: A TALE OF THE FRENCH REVOLU-
TION, Macmillan. *Gertrude Demain Hammond.* 1916]. [1884]
CHRISTMAS-TREE LAND. Macmillan. *Walter Crane.* 1884
US: AN OLD-FASHIONED STORY. Macmillan.
Walter Crane. 1885
A CHARGE FULFILLED. S.P.C.K. *R. Caton Wood-
ville*. [1886]
SILVERTHORNS. Hatchards. *J. Noel Paton*. [1886]
FOUR WINDS FARM. Macmillan. *Walter Crane.* [1886]. 1887
MARRYING AND GIVING IN MARRIAGE. Long-
mans. 1887
THE ABBEY BY THE SEA. S.P.C.K. *Frank Dadd*. [1887]
THE PALACE IN THE GARDEN. Hatchards. *Harriet
M. Bennett*. 1887
LITTLE MISS PEGGY: ONLY A NURSERY STORY.
Macmillan. *Walter Crane*. 1887
FOUR GHOST STORIES. Macmillan. 1888
FIVE MINUTES' STORIES. S.P.C.K. *Gordon Browne,*
etc. [1888]
THE THIRD MISS ST. QUENTIN. Hatchards. [1888]
A CHRISTMAS POSY. Macmillan. *Walter Crane.* 1888
FRENCH LIFE IN LETTERS. Macmillan's Primary
Series of French, etc. 1889
THAT GIRL IN BLACK, AND BRONZIE. Chatto and
Windus. 1889

NESTA: OR FRAGMENTS OF A LITTLE LIFE.
Chambers. [*B. Foster.*]? 1889
NEIGHBOURS. Hatchards. *Mary Ellen Edwards.* 1889
GREAT UNCLE HOOT-TOOT. S.P.C.K. *Gordon Browne,* and others. [1889]
THE OLD PINCUSHION, or AUNT CLOTILDA'S GUESTS. Griffith Farran. *Mrs Adrian Hope (Laura M. Trowbridge)* [Farran. *Mabel and Edith Taylor.* n.d. Chambers. *Mabel Lucie Attwell.* 1910] [1889]
A HOUSE TO LET. S.P.C.K. *W. J. Morgan.* [1889]
THE RECTORY CHILDREN. Macmillan. *Walter Crane.* 1889
LITTLE MOTHER BUNCH. Cassell. *Mary Ellen Edwards.* [Cassell. *Elizabeth Earnshaw.* n.d.] 1890
THE GREEN CASKET, AND OTHER STORIES. Chambers. *Robert Barnes, W. J. Morgan.* [1890]
TWELVE TINY TALES. S.P.C.K. *W. J. Morgan.* [1890]
FAMILY TROUBLES. S.P.C.K. *W. J. Morgan.* [1890]
THE STORY OF A SPRING MORNING, AND OTHER STORIES. Longmans. *Mary Ellen Edwards.* [Chambers. *Molly Benatar.* n.d. (*c.* 1920)] [1890]
THE CHILDREN OF THE CASTLE. Macmillan. *Walter Crane.* 1890
THE RED GRANGE. Methuen. *Gordon Browne.* 1891
SWEET CONTENT. Griffith Farran. *W. Rainey.* [Chambers. *A. S. Boyd.* 1908] 1891
THE BEWITCHED LAMP. Chambers. *Robert Barnes.* [1891]
THE LUCKY DUCKS, AND OTHER STORIES. S.P.C.K. *W. J. Morgan.* [1891]
NURSE HEATHERDALE'S STORY. Macmillan. *L. Leslie Brooke.* 1891
THE MAN WITH THE PAN PIPES, AND OTHER STORIES. S.P.C.K. *W. J. Morgan.* [1892]
LEONA. Cassell. 1892
AN ENCHANTED GARDEN: FAIRY STORIES. Unwin. *W. J. Hennessy.* 1892
IMOGEN, or ONLY EIGHTEEN. Chambers. *Herbert A. Bone.* 1892
STORIES OF THE SAINTS FOR CHILDREN. Longmans. [*Traditional Woodcuts*] 1892
FARTHINGS: THE STORY OF A STRAY AND A WAIF. Gardner, Darton. *G. M. Broadley.* 1892

ROBIN REDBREAST, A STORY FOR GIRLS.
Chambers. *Robert Barnes.* [1892]

THE GIRLS AND I: A VERACIOUS HISTORY.
Macmillan. *L. Leslie Brooke.* 1892

STUDIES AND STORIES. A. D. Innes. *Walter Crane.* 1893

THE NEXT-DOOR HOUSE. Chambers. *W. Hatherell.* [1893]

THE THIRTEEN LITTLE BLACK PIGS, AND
OTHER STORIES. S.P.C.K. *W. J. Morgan.* [1893]

MARY: A NURSERY STORY FOR VERY LITTLE
CHILDREN. Macmillan. *L. Leslie Brooke.* 1893

BLANCHE: A STORY FOR GIRLS. Chambers.
R. Barnes. [1893] 1894

MY NEW HOME. Macmillan. *L. Leslie Brooke.* 1894

OLIVIA: A STORY FOR GIRLS. Chambers. *R. Barnes.*
[1894] 1895

OPPOSITE NEIGHBOURS, AND OTHER STORIES.
S.P.C.K. *W. J. Morgan.* [1895]

THE CARVED LIONS. Macmillan. *L. Leslie Brooke.*
[Pilot press (Victorian Tales for Girls) 1947. Faith Press.
Geoffrey Rhoades. 1960]. 1895

WHITE TURRETS. Chambers. *W. Rainey.* [1895] 1896

FRIENDLY JOEY, AND OTHER STORIES. S.P.C.K. [1896]
W. J. Morgan.

UNCANNY TALES. Hutchinson. *Fred Hyland.*
[decorations] [1896]

THE ORIEL WINDOW. Macmillan. *L. Leslie Brooke.* 1896

PHILLIPA. Chambers. *J. Finnemore.* [1896] 1897

STORIES FOR CHILDREN IN ILLUSTRATION OF
THE LORD'S PRAYER. Gardner Darton. *Gordon
Browne, M. E. Edwards, W. H. C. Groome,* and others. 1897

MEG LANGHOME, or THE DAY AFTER TOMOR-
ROW. Chambers. *W. Rainey.* 1897

MISS MOUSE AND HER BOYS. Macmillan. *L. Leslie
Brooke.* 1897

THE LAUREL WALK. Isbister. 1898

GREYLING TOWERS: A STORY FOR THE YOUNG.
Chambers. *Percy Tarrant.* 1898

THE MAGIC NUTS. Macmillan. *Rosie M. M. Pitman.* 1898

THE GRIM HOUSE. Nisbet. *Warwick Goble.* 1899

THIS AND THAT: A TALE OF TWO TINIES. Macmillan. *Hugh Thomson.* 1899

THE CHILDREN'S HOUR. Nelson. [Illustrations signed "C.P.R.", "E.L.", "A.D."] [1899]

THE THREE WITCHES. Chambers. *Lewis Baumer.* [1900]

THE HOUSE THAT GREW. Macmillan. *Alice B. Woodward.* 1900

MY PRETTY AND HER LITTLE BROTHER TOO, AND OTHER STORIES. Chambers. *Lewis Baumer.* [1901]

THE BLUE BABY, AND OTHER STORIES. Unwin. *Maud C. Forster.* [Chambers (with other stories). *Lewis Baumer* [1904]]. [1901]

THE WOOD-PIGEONS AND MARY. Macmillan. *H. R. Millar.* 1901

PETERKIN. Macmillan. *H. R. Millar.* 1902

THE MYSTERY OF THE PINEWOOD and HOLLOW TREE HOUSE. Nister. *A. A. Dixon.* [1903]

THE RUBY RING. Macmillan. *Rosie M. M. Pitman.* 1904

THE BOLTED DOOR, AND OTHER STORIES. Chambers. *Lewis Baumer.* [1906]

THE WRONG ENVELOPE, AND OTHER STORIES. Macmillan. 1906

JASPER: A STORY FOR CHILDREN. Macmillan. *Gertrude Demain Hammond.* 1906

THE LITTLE GUEST: A STORY FOR CHILDREN. Macmillan. *Gertrude Demain Hammond.* 1907

FAIRIES—OF SORTS. Macmillan. *Gertrude Demain Hammond.* 1908

THE FEBRUARY BOYS: A STORY FOR CHILDREN Chambers. *Mabel Lucie Attwell.* 1909

THE STORY OF A YEAR. Macmillan. *Gertrude Demain Hammond.* 1910

FAIRIES AFIELD. Macmillan. *Gertrude Demain Hammond.* 1911

Nearly all the short stories and many of the long ones (other than those published by Macmillan) appeared first in various periodicals, notably *Aunt Judy's Magazine, Little Folks, The Child's Pictorial, Atalanta, The Monthly Packet* and *The Newberry House Magazine.* The title LEO'S POST OFFICE, which may be found in catalogues, is not a new book but a reprint of two stories from THE GREEN CASKET (1890) made by Chambers in 1895.

In 1957 the Harvill Press published a volume called FAIRY

STORIES BY MRS. MOLESWORTH, edited by Roger Lancelyn Green. This contains 'The Reel Fairies' from TELL ME A STORY; 'The Story of a King's Daughter' from CHRISTMAS-TREE LAND; 'The Summer Princess' and 'The Magic Rose' from AN ENCHANTED GARDEN; 'Princess Ice-Heart' from STUDIES AND STORIES; 'The Weather Maiden' from FAIRIES AFIELD, and the hitherto uncollected story 'The Magic Spinning Wheel', for which see section IIA. below.

Two volumes in Dent's Children's Illustrated Classics, both edited by Roger Lancelyn Green, contain reprints of stories by Mrs. Molesworth: MODERN FAIRY STORIES (1955) contains 'The Summer Princess' from AN ENCHANTED GARDEN, and TALES OF MAKE-BELIEVE (1960) contains 'The Six Poor Little Princesses' from A CHRISTMAS POSY.

A GOLDEN LAND (1958), Constable, edited by James Reeves, contains 'The Swallows' from SUMMER STORIES FOR BOYS AND GIRLS.

II. UNCOLLECTED ITEMS BY MRS MOLESWORTH SO FAR DISCOVERED

A. Uncollected Short Stories for Children.
THE FAIRY WITH TWO VOICES. *Child's Pictorial*: Dec. 1886.
LOST, STOLEN OR STRAYED. *Jack Frost's Little Prisoners.* (Skeffington) 1887.
CHERI'S SECOND ESCAPADE. *Stories Jolly, Stories New.* (Skeffington) 1889.
A SMALL PARCEL. *Please Tell Me Another Tale.* (Skeffington) 1890.
THE MAGIC SPINNING-WHEEL. *Told by the Fire-side.* (Griffith Farran) [1890].
AN ODD FANCY. *Child's Pictorial*: July 1892.
SPICED GINGERBREAD. *Now For a Story.* (Skeffington) 1893.
THE FIGHTING FLOWERS. *The Talking Clock* (Ernest Nister). [1893].
PAUL'S BLUEBELLS. *The Child's Pictorial*: Feb. 1893.
THE SNOW WITCH. *A Cosy Corner* (Ernest Nister). [1893].
AUNTIE'S DINNER PARTY. *The Story Shop* (Ernest Nister). [1895].

NOT QUITE TRUE. *Nister's Holiday Annual.* 1898.
THE THIRSTY HORSES. With *The Next Door Children* by
    Geraldine R. Glasgow. [Date unascertainable].
    Note: Several of the above stories appear in later collections
issued, usually undated, by Ernest Nister.

"THAT KISS OF YOURS": A STORY *NOT* FOR THE
    YOUNG. *Time.* Dec. 1888.

B.   Uncollected Articles.
THE BEST BOOKS FOR CHILDREN. *Pall Mall Gazette*:
    29 Oct. 1887.
THE ART OF AUTHORSHIP, edited by George Bainton
    [contribution by Mrs. Molesworth]. 1890.
FOR THE LITTLE ONES. *Woman's Mission*, edited by Baroness
    Burdett Coutts. 1893.
ON THE ART OF WRITING FICTION FOR CHILDREN.
    Atalanta: May, 1893.
HOW I WRITE MY CHILDREN'S STORIES. *Little Folks*:
    July, 1894.
STORY-WRITING. *The Monthly Packet*: Aug. 1894.
A CRY FROM THE FAR WEST. *Macmillan's Magazine*: Dec.
    1897.
STORY-READING AND STORY-WRITING. *Chambers's
    Journals*: 5 Nov. 1898.
PRINCE'S MEADOWS, or POVERTY CORNER. Being a
    Short Account of the Royal Waterloo Hospital for Children
    and Women. [Twenty-one page pamphlet]. 1907.

C.   Uncollected Poems.
NATURE AND LOVE. *Tinsley's Magazine*: Aug. 1875.
THANKS. *Little Wide-Awake.* Feb. 1881.
A RACE. *Child's Pictorial.* April, 1888: TWELVE TINY TALES
    1890. [Reprinted in THE BOOK OF NONSENSE. Dent: 1956]
SECRETS. *Child's Pictorial:* May, 1888. *Buttercups and Daisies*
    (Nister). [1894].
WHITE SAND AND GREY SAND. *Little Folks*: Jan. 1894.
CHAIRS TO MEND. *Little Folks*: April, 1894.
KNIVES AND SCISSORS TO GRIND. *Little Folks*: May, 1894.
STARWBERRIES, SCARLET STRAWBERRIES. *Little Folks*:
    July, 1894.

III. WRITINGS ABOUT MRS MOLESWORTH

There are very few of these, and the biographical details contained in them are not always accurate. A full-length Biography by Miss Ruth Robertson is in preparation.

JUVENILE LITERATURE AS IT IS. Edward Salmon. 1888.

A POPULAR WRITER FOR CHILDREN: MRS. MOLESWORTH. "F.H.L." *Westminster Budget*. 20 Oct. 1893.

SOME WOMEN NOVELISTS: MRS. MOLESWORTH. Sarah A. Tooley. *The Woman at Home*. Dec. 1987.

MRS. MOLESWORTH. Bella Sydney Woolf. *The Quiver* (Vol. 41, pp. 674-6). June, 1906.

OBITUARY: MRS. MOLESWORTH. Anonymous. *The Times*. 22 July, 1921.

TELLERS OF TALES. Roger Lancelyn Green. 1946; 1956.

MRS. EWING, MRS. MOLESWORTH, AND MRS. HODGSON BURNETT. Marghanita Laski. 1950.

NOTES ON MRS. MOLESWORTH. Roger Lancelyn Green. *Times Literary Supplement*. 17 Nov. 1950.

MRS. MOLESWORTH AND HER BOOKS. Roger Lancelyn Green. *The Library World*. Nov. 1951.

MRS. MOLESWORTH. Roger Lancelyn Green. *The Junior Bookshelf*. July, 1957.

IV. AMERICAN EDITIONS OF
BOOKS BY AND ABOUT MRS MOLESWORTH

'CARROTS' JUST A LITTLE BOY. St. Martin's. *Walter Crane*. 1957.

THE CUCKOO CLOCK. Dutton. *Ernest H. Shepard*. 1954. St. Martin's. *C. E. Brock*. 1877.

THE TAPESTRY ROOM. Random. *Walter Crane*. 1961.

TELLERS OF TALES. Roger Lancelyn Green. Dufour. 1958.